alphabet cooking

quadrille

K
is for korean

recipes by rukmini iyer
photography by kim lightbody

TRADITIONAL

KIMCHI BOKEUM BAB

SOONDUBU JJIGAE

KIMCHI JJIGAE

SEAWEED 2.00

G MSAHAMNIDA

K is for Korean contains 50 of the most definitive

and delicious recipes in modern Korean cooking.

K is for Korean ingredients

adzuki (aduki) beans are prepared sweet red beans commonly used in Korean desserts

Korean pear (bae) are a species of pear native to East Asia

chunjang is a Korean black bean paste

dangmyeon are glass noodles

doenjang is a soybean paste which literally means 'thick sauce' in Korean

garaetteok is a cylindrical Korean rice cake

gim (kim) is an edible type of Korean seaweed

gochujang is a Korean red pepper paste

gochugaru are Korean red pepper flakes

gosari (dried) are young stems of bracken which are the main wild edible greens eaten in Korea

jujube (daechu) are sweet red dates

kimchi is a traditional Korean dish made from fermented vegetables

mandu is a type of Korean dumpling, they are similar to *pelmeni* and *pierogi* in Slavic cultures.

Korean radish (mu) are much larger than the common radish and have a milder flavour and spice (also known as a daikon radish)

myeolchi are Korean dried anchovies

patbingsu tteok is a soft mini rice cake for patbingsu (shaved ice dessert)

perilla leaves *see* perilla seeds (below)

perilla seeds is a herb from the mint family

saeujeot is fermented shrimp

somen noodles are very thin white Japanese noodles

ssamjang sauce is a spicy paste made from made of doenjang, gochujang, sesame oil, garlic, onions and sugar

(Many Korean ingredients are now available from larger supermarkets which are starting to stock more specific ingredients. However, it is also worth shopping at your nearest Asian supermarket for the harder-to-find ingredients.)

人접시 (small plates)

01

haemul pajeon

(pancakes with spring onions)

ingredients

1 clove garlic, minced
2.5cm (1in) ginger, minced
150g (5½oz/1¼ cups)
  plain (all-purpose) flour
30g (1oz) rice flour
15g (½oz) cornflour (cornstarch)
1 tsp baking powder
1 tsp sea salt
2 eggs, lightly beaten
1 bunch (140–150g/5–5½oz)
  spring onions (scallions), sliced
  in half, then lengthways
170g (6oz) mixed seafood
1 Tbsp vegetable oil

1 Tbsp vinegar
1 Tbsp soy sauce
1 Tbsp sesame oil
1 Tbsp gochujang
½ tsp caster (superfine) sugar

mix

Mix the garlic, ginger, flours, baking powder and
salt together in a large bowl, before whisking in the
eggs and 150ml (5fl oz/⅔ cup) cold water.

beat

Beat until you have a smooth batter, then add in
the spring onions and seafood.

heat

Heat the vegetable oil in a large frying pan until very
hot, then lower the heat and spoon in half of the
batter. Fry on a medium heat for 2 minutes on each
side, transferring to a plate lined with kitchen paper,
then repeat with the remaining batter.

whisk

Meanwhile, make the dipping sauce by whisking
together the vinegar, soy sauce, sesame oil,
gochujang and sugar. Serve alongside the
hot pancakes.

gimbap

(beef sushi rolls)

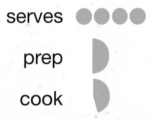

serves ●●●●

prep

cook

ingredients

150g (5½oz/⅔ cup) sushi rice
4 Tbsp sesame oil
1 red (bell) pepper, sliced into
thin strips
2 cloves garlic, finely chopped
100g (3½oz) spinach
2.5cm (1in) ginger, finely
chopped
100g (3½oz) minced
(ground) beef
1 Tbsp soy sauce
salt and freshly ground black
pepper
2 sheets gim
1 avocado, peeled and sliced
into strips

boil

Add the rice to a pan of boiling salted water and
boil for 12–13 minutes before draining it well.
Return the drained rice to the pan, cover and allow
to steam dry for a further 20 minutes (off the heat).

heat

Meanwhile, heat 1 tablespoon of the sesame oil in
a large frying pan and add the pepper. Fry for 6–7
minutes over a low heat, stirring frequently, until
softened. Season well with salt, then set aside.

fry

In the same frying pan, heat another tablespoon
of sesame oil with half of the chopped garlic.
Add the spinach and stir-fry for 1–2 minutes until
just wilted. Season well with salt, and set aside
with the pepper.

heat

Heat another tablespoon of the sesame oil in the same frying pan, and add the remaining half of the garlic and chopped ginger. Add the minced beef, and stir-fry for 5–6 minutes until broken up and cooked through. Season with the soy sauce and freshly ground pepper and set aside.

stir

Stir a pinch of salt and the remaining tablespoon of sesame oil through the hot rice.

make

To make the gimbap, place a sheet of gim on a sushi rolling mat, shiny side down. Spread over half the rice, leaving a 5-cm (2-in) border on one side, and pat it down well with the back of a spoon. In alternate lines, vertical to the border, place lines of the avocado, red pepper, spinach and minced beef.

turn

Turn the rolling mat so that the 5-cm (2-in) border is furthest away from you. Carefully, roll the seaweed up in the mat to form a cylinder, pressing the rice together through the mat. Finish by rolling the rice log over onto the border to seal.

cut

Place the rolls on a chopping board, and cut into 2–3-cm (¾–1-in) slices with a very sharp knife. Eat immediately, or cover and refrigerate.

03

bokkeum
(stir fry)

serves

prep

marinate

cook

ingredients
1 Tbsp gochugaru
1 Tbsp gochujang
2 Tbsp soy sauce
1 Tbsp sesame oil
2.5cm (1in) ginger, minced
2 cloves garlic, minced
½ green chilli, finely chopped
2 spring onions (scallions),
   finely sliced
1 tsp sesame seeds
180g (6½oz) raw king prawns
1 Tbsp vegetable oil

hot rice or lettuce leaves,
   to serve

mix
Mix the gochugaru, gochujang, soy sauce, sesame oil, ginger, garlic, chilli, spring onions and sesame seeds together, and then stir through the prawns. Cover and leave to marinate for 15 minutes.

heat
Heat the vegetable oil in a large wok, then add the prawns. Stir-fry for 2–3 minutes until cooked through, then serve immediately. Serve with rice or lettuce leaves.

gyeran jjim

(steamed egg casserole)

serves

prep

cook

ingredients

4 eggs
1 Tbsp fish sauce or Korean
   salted shrimp sauce
1 tsp sea salt
3 spring onions (scallions), finely
   chopped

boil

Fill a saucepan with water to come up to 5cm (2in) deep. Bring to the boil, covered with a tightly fitting lid.

whisk

Meanwhile, whisk together the eggs, 200ml (7fl oz/scant 1 cup) water, fish sauce and salt for 1 minute, until fluffy. Stir through half the spring onions.

transfer

Transfer the egg mixture into one large or two small bowls that will fit comfortably in the saucepan with the water. Place the bowls on a piece of folded foil, then lower carefully into the pan. Replace the lid, reduce the heat to a simmer, and steam for 10 minutes.

scatter

Scatter the remaining spring onions over the steamed eggs, then replace the lid and cook for a further minute. Serve immediately.

gaeran mari
(omelette roll)
(omelette roll)

ingredients

4 eggs
pinch salt
1 tsp vegetable oil
2 spring onions (scallions),
 finely chopped
1 sheet gim

whisk

In a bowl, whisk the eggs along with a pinch of salt until smooth.

heat

Heat the oil in a medium-sized frying pan and pour the eggs in evenly, before scattering over the chopped spring onions. Let the omelette cook on a very low heat for 5–7 minutes, until you can see that the edges are just set and the middle is opaque.

place

Place the gim sheet over the eggs, then carefully, fold the omelette over on itself four or five times. Pat it down gently with a spatula as you roll it, then transfer it to a chopping board.

cool

Allow the omelette to cool down for a few minutes, before carefully slicing into 1.5-cm (½-in) slices. Serve hot or cold.

mandu

(dumplings)

make ●●●●

prep

cook

ingredients

400g (14oz/3¼ cups) plain
(all-purpose) flour
1 tsp salt
2 tsp vegetable oil

2 dried shiitake mushrooms
300g (10½oz) minced
(ground) beef
150g (5½oz) minced
(ground) pork
70g (2½oz/⅓ cup) tofu, finely
chopped
90g (3oz) napa cabbage,
finely chopped
2 spring onions (scallions),
finely chopped
25g (1oz/½ cup) chives, finely
chopped
2 cloves garlic, minced
2.5cm (1in) ginger, minced
2 Tbsp sesame oil
2 Tbsp sea salt

mix

To make the gyoza wrappers, combine the flour
and salt in a bowl, then pour in the 160ml (5½fl
oz/⅔ cup) water and vegetable oil. Mix together
with a fork until combined, then use your hands to
briefly knead together into a soft dough. The dough
may look dry depending on your flour, so add a
few more drops of water if needed. Roll into a ball,
cover in clingfilm (plastic wrap), then leave it to rest
at room temperature for 10 minutes.

soak

Soak the shiitake mushrooms in boiling water for
5 minutes, then chop finely. Combine them with all
the remaining filling ingredients in a large bowl, then
mix thoroughly with the sesame oil and sea salt.
Fry off a small piece of the filling in a hot frying pan,
and taste to check the seasoning. Add more salt to
your taste.

➡➡➡

➡ ➡ ➡
2 Tbsp soy sauce
1 Tbsp sesame oil
1 Tbsp rice wine
1 Tbsp gochujang

divide

Divide the dough in half, then in half again until you have 16 pieces. Roll each into a ball and keep under clingfilm while you roll each out into a 15-cm (6-in) circle.

fill

Place a golf ball-sized portion of filling on one side of each circle. Brush a little water along the edges, then fold the dumpling into a half-moon shape. You can leave the dumplings shaped like this, or alternatively, sit the half moon so that the folded edge is at the top, then bring the sides around the centre tightly, using a little more water to secure them into the shape overleaf. Continue until you have used up all the dough. The filling will make double the quantity of dumplings, so you can freeze the extra filling (you can also use the mixture to make Wanja Jeon, see page 30.)

heat

Heat water to a depth of 5cm (2in) in a steamer and line the centre with a circle of baking (parchment) paper. Place the dumplings in the steamer in a single layer and steam for 10 minutes, until the filling is cooked through.

whisk

Meanwhile, make the sauce by whisking together the soy sauce, sesame oil, rice wine, 1 tablespoon water and gochujang in a little bowl. Serve alongside the hot dumplings for dipping.

dubu jorim

(fried tofu)

serves

prep

cook

ingredients
350g (12½oz) firm tofu
1 Tbsp vegetable oil
2 Tbsp soy sauce
1 Tbsp sesame oil
1 clove garlic, finely minced
½ tsp caster (superfine) sugar
1 tsp gochugaru
1 tsp sesame seeds
1 spring onion (scallion),
   finely sliced

slice
Slice the tofu into 1-cm (½-in) slices and pat dry.

heat
Heat the vegetable oil in a large frying pan. Place the tofu pieces in the pan in a single layer, and fry on a medium heat for 4 minutes on each side, until golden-brown. Carefully flip over and fry for 4 minutes more.

mix
Meanwhile, mix together the soy sauce, 2 tablespoons water, sesame oil, garlic, sugar, gochugaru, sesame seeds and spring onion. Spoon the sauce over each piece of tofu, then simmer for a further 5 minutes on a low heat, until the sauce has reduced. Arrange the tofu on a small dish and serve hot or cold.

yukhoe

(seasoned raw beef)

ingredients

250g (9oz) fillet beef steak
  (ultra fresh)
1 Tbsp pine nuts
1 Tbsp sesame seeds
1 Tbsp sesame oil
1 Tbsp soy sauce
1cm (½in) ginger, finely minced
1 clove garlic, finely minced
1 tsp freshly ground black
  pepper
½ tsp sea salt

1 Korean pear, cut into
  matchsticks, to serve
2 quails eggs, yolks only, to
  serve

slice

Slice the beef into 2-mm (1/12- in) strips, and place in a bowl along with the pine nuts and sesame seeds.

mix

Mix the sesame oil, soy sauce, ginger, garlic and black pepper together in a small bowl, and then stir through the beef.

serve

Place a half of the Korean pear on each plate, and top with a neat circle of the beef. Make a small indentation with a teaspoon and place a whole egg yolk on each, either in the shell or directly into the beef. Serve immediately.

09

wanja jeon

(mini beef burgers)

serves

prep

cook

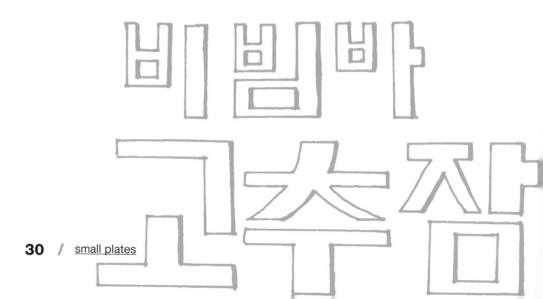

ingredients

200g (7oz) firm tofu
500g (1lb 2oz) minced
  (ground) beef
2 Tbsp sesame oil
2 spring onions (scallions),
  finely chopped
2 cloves garlic, finely minced
1–2 tsp sea salt
generous grind black pepper
50g (1¾oz/heaped ⅓ cup) plain
  (all-purpose) flour
2 Tbsp vegetable oil
2 eggs
1 tsp sea salt

blitz

Blitz the tofu in a food processor until well broken
up, then combine with the beef, sesame oil, spring
onions, garlic, sea salt and black pepper. If you
wish to check the seasoning, fry off a small piece
of the mixture in a hot frying pan until cooked
through, then taste and season as needed.

divide

Divide the mixture in half, then half again until you
have 16 equally sized pieces. Flatten each into a
small, round burger, no thicker than 1.5cm (½in),
and dip each into the flour.

make

Preheat your oven to 50°C/122°F. Heat one
tablespoon of the vegetable oil in a large frying pan.
Whisk the eggs with the salt then dip each floured
burger into the egg mixture before transferring it
directly into the pan.

fry

Fry the patties for 5 minutes on each side on a
medium heat until cooked through, then transfer to
a plate lined with kitchen paper. Keep warm in the
oven. Add a little more oil to the pan, and continue
until the burgers are all cooked. These are delicious
served hot or cold.

SMALL DISHES

O T B	SALAD	4.50
GIMARI	SALAD	4.50
CHICKEN	KUNMANDU	3.60
SHRIMP	KUNMANDU	3.90
SEAWEED	SALAD	3.90
PRAWN	SALAD	4.90
NOODLE	SALAD	
BROCCOLI	SALAD	3.90

ON THE BAB

BIBIMBAB
RICE
BUNS
ROLL

YANGYUM CHICKEN   S   M   L

SPECIAL	SOY
SWEET	SPICY
GARLIC	MAYO
SPRING	ONION

5.50   11.90   21.90

TRADITIONAL

KIMCHI BOKEUM
SOONDUBU JJIGAE
KIMCHI JJIGAE

SIDE   KIMCHI 2.00   DANMUJI 2.00   RICE 2.00   SEAWEED 2.00

THANK YOU   G MSAHAMN

tteokbokki

(spicy rice cake)

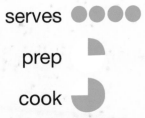

serves ●●●●

prep

cook

ingredients

600g (1lb 5oz) cylindrical rice
cakes (garaetteok), defrosted
if frozen
500ml (17fl oz/generous 2 cups)
anchovy broth (see page 119)
or fish stock
70g (2½oz) gochujang
1 Tbsp gochugaru
1 tsp caster (superfine) sugar
3 spring onions (scallions),
finely sliced
1 Tbsp sesame oil
sea salt

soak

Soak the rice cakes in a bowl of water for 15
minutes before using.

make

Make up the anchovy broth. Strain through a sieve
into a clean saucepan. Bring to the boil, taste and
season with sea salt as needed.

drain

Drain the rice cakes and add to the broth, along
with the gochujang, gochugaru and sugar.

boil

Bring to the boil and simmer for 15 minutes, stirring
frequently. Stir through the spring onions and drizzle
over the sesame oil just before serving.

wang mandu

(pork dumplings)

ingredients

1 tsp active dry (fast-action) yeast
1 Tbsp vegetable oil
½ tsp caster (superfine) sugar
250g (9oz/2 cups) strong white bread flour
½ tsp sea salt
1 Tbsp sesame oil
1 cloves garlic, finely minced
2.5cm (1in) ginger, finely minced
½ onion, finely chopped
1 courgette (zucchini) (approx.100g/3½oz) finely chopped
50g (1¾oz) chestnut mushrooms, finely chopped
1 tsp sea salt
250g (9oz) minced (ground) pork

2 Tbsp soy sauce, plus extra to serve

mix

Whisk together 125ml (4fl oz/½ cup) warm water, yeast, vegetable oil and sugar in a mixing jug. Sift the flour and salt together in a large bowl.

pour

Pour the yeast mixture over the flour and work together until it forms a stiff dough. Tip onto a work surface and knead for 4–5 minutes, then return to the bowl, cover and leave to rise for 1 hour 30 minutes, until it has doubled in size.

heat

Heat the sesame oil in a large frying pan, and add the garlic, ginger, onion, courgette and mushrooms. Fry on a medium heat for 10 minutes, until softened, then stir through the salt. Tip into a bowl and allow to cool.

mix

Mix the pork into the cooked vegetables along with the soy sauce, and fry off a small portion in a pan to check the seasoning. Adjust according to taste and set aside.

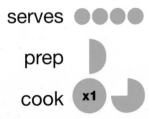

serves ●●●●

prep

cook x1

knead

Punch down the dough, knead it briefly, then return
it to the bowl to rest for a further 15 minutes.

divide

Divide the dough into 8 portions and roll each
of these into a flat round, around 11cm (4¼in)
in diameter. Place a tablespoon of pork filling in
the centre, then twist up the tops together tightly,
using a little water to seal. Place on a piece of
baking (parchment) paper, and continue until all 8
dumplings are made up, each on a piece of paper.

steam

Fill a saucepan with a depth of 5–7.5cm (2–3in)
water and bring to the boil. Place a steamer basket
over the top. Arrange the dumplings inside, cover,
and steam for 15 minutes.

serve

Serve hot, with good-quality soy sauce on
the side.

념
(condiments)

kimchi
(pickled cabbage)

ingredients

1 napa cabbage

50g (1¾oz/⅓ cup) sea salt

5 cloves garlic, grated

5cm (2in) ginger, grated

3 Tbsp gochugaru

100ml (3½fl oz/scant 1 cup)
    fish sauce

350g (12½oz) Korean or daikon
    radish, cut into 2.5-cm (1-in)
    matchsticks

5 spring onions (scallions),
    sliced into 5-mm (¼-in) rounds

wash

Wash the cabbage thoroughly in plenty of cold water, then slice in half lengthways. Cut each half lengthways again into long quarters and then a final time into eighths, making sure to keep the stem intact.

sprinkle

Sprinkle each piece with the sea salt, making sure to work the salt in between all the leaves, then place all the cabbage pieces in a large bowl. Pour over just enough cold water to cover the cabbage, arrange a plate on top and weigh it down with a couple of tins. Leave for 2 hours to brine.

mix

Meanwhile, make the marinade by mixing together the garlic, ginger, gochugaru, fish sauce, radish and spring onions until well combined. Set aside.

drain

Once the cabbage has sat in the brine for 2 hours, drain it well in a colander, then rinse for several minutes under cold running water. Shake off the excess water in the colander, then gently squeeze the leaves to remove as much water as possible. Place the drained leaves in a large bowl, pour over the marinade, then using your hands (plastic gloves recommended), work the paste well into each layer of leaf.

fill

Pack the marinated leaves into a 1-litre (34fl oz/4 cups) Mason jar or non-reactive (e.g. glass) container, press them down well with the back of a metal spoon and cover.

ferment

Leave for 5 days at room temperature. The cabbage will become submerged in a red liquid – use the back of a spoon to press the leaves down under the liquid each day before replacing the lid. After 5 days, refrigerate the kimchi and allow it to mature for a further 2–3 weeks. It will keep well for a couple of months refrigerated and its strength willl increase the longer it is left.

kkakdugi
(radish kimchi)

serves **10**

prep

salt

ferment **4 days**

ingredients

450g (1lb) Korean or daikon
   radish, cut into 1.5-cm
   (½-in) cubes
½ Tbsp salt
½ Tbsp caster (superfine) sugar
2 cloves garlic, minced
2.5cm (1in) ginger, minced
2 Tbsp gochugaru
3 Tbsp fish sauce
1 spring onion (scallion),
   finely chopped

season

Place the radish cubes in a large bowl and sprinkle with the salt and sugar. Mix well, then leave to sit for 1 hour. Drain the radish cubes well, shaking off all the excess water.

mix

Mix the garlic, ginger, gochugaru, fish sauce and spring onion together in a bowl, and set aside. Mix the radish with the mixture until evenly covered, then pack tightly into a 500ml (17fl oz/2 cups) glass jar, making sure to press down evenly to remove any pockets of air between the radish pieces.

store

Cover and store at room temperature for 24 hours, before transferring to the fridge to ferment for a further 3–4 days before eating. This will store well in the fridge for 1–2 months.

oi
muchim
(pickled cucumber)

serves 10-15

prep

marinate over-night

cook

ingredients
2 Tbsp white vinegar
50g (1¾oz) sea salt
700g (1lb 9oz) pickling
   cucumbers

1 Tbsp sesame oil
1 Tbsp soy sauce
1 spring onion (scallion),
   finely sliced
1 clove garlic minced
1 tsp gochugaru
1 tsp sesame seeds

heat
Heat 700ml (23½fl oz/scant 3 cups) water, vinegar and sea salt in a saucepan and bring to the boil, stirring until the salt has dissolved. Place the cucumbers in a 1.4-litre (47-fl oz/6¼-cup) glass jar, pour over the brine, seal and leave to cool down. Refrigerate overnight.

slice
The next day, just before you are ready to eat, remove 4–5 cucumbers from the brine and finely slice. Mix together the sesame oil, soy sauce, spring onion, garlic, gochugaru and sesame seeds. Toss through the sliced cucumber and then serve immediately.

store
Keep the remaining whole pickled cucumbers in the fridge for 2–3 weeks, removing them as you wish to make the spicy version of the pickle by combining each time with the sauce ingredients.

ojinguh jut

(fermented squid)

serves **6-8**

prep

ferment **2 weeks**

ingredients

200g (7oz) squid, cleaned
3 tsp sea salt
2.5cm (1in) ginger, finely minced
2 cloves garlic, finely minced
2 spring onions (scallions),
    finely chopped
2 Tbsp gochujang
1 Tbsp gochugaru
2 Tbsp fish sauce
1 Tbsp rice vinegar

slice

Slice the squid into rings and then mix well with the sea salt. Cover and refrigerate for 1 hour.

drain

Drain the squid, then place in a 300ml (10fl oz/ 1¼ cups) jar or tightly fitting container and refrigerate overnight.

mix

The next day, combine the ginger, garlic, spring onions, gochujang, gochugaru, fish sauce and rice vinegar. Mix well through the squid, then return to the fridge and leave, covered, for one week.

stir

Stir the squid after a week, then cover and refrigerate again for another week. Eat within the next month.

manul changachi

(pickled garlic)

serves **8**

prep

cook

mature 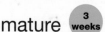 **3 weeks**

ingredients

200ml (7fl oz/scant 1 cup)
  soy sauce
60ml (2fl oz/¼ cup) vinegar
60g (2oz/generous ¼ cup)
  caster (superfine) sugar
4 bulbs garlic

boil

Place the soy sauce, vinegar and sugar in a saucepan and bring to the boil. Simmer for 10 minutes on a low heat.

peel

Meanwhile, divide up the garlic bulbs and peel the cloves. Place the peeled cloves in a 250-ml (8½-fl oz/1-cup) jam jar.

store

Leave the reduced soy mixture to cool to room temperature and then pour it over the garlic cloves. Make sure they are completely submerged in the liquid, then cover and leave at room temperature for 3 weeks to pickle, before refrigerating. These will last for three months in the refrigerator.

47 /

반찬

(sides and salads)

gaji namul

(steamed aubergine)

serves ●●

prep ▶

cook ▶

ingredients

1 aubergine (eggplant)
1 Tbsp sesame oil
1 Tbsp soy sauce
1 clove garlic, minced
2 tsp gochugaru
1 Tbsp sesame seeds
1 spring onion (scallion),
  finely chopped

slice

Slice the aubergine into thirds, then across into 1-cm (½-in) slices, then across again so you have short rectangular sticks, approximately 5cm (2in) by 1cm (½in).

steam

Fill a pan with water to come a depth of 5–7.5cm (2–3in) and bring to the boil. Place a steamer basket over the top. Arrange the aubergine sticks in a single layer, cover, and steam for 7 minutes, until the aubergine is cooked through.

whisk

Meanwhile, whisk together the sesame oil, soy sauce, garlic, gochugaru, sesame seeds and spring onion.

dress

Once the aubergine is cooked, toss with the dressing and serve hot, scattered with extra sesame seeds if you wish.

Korean coleslaw

serves ●●●●●●

prep ◢

ingredients

2 large carrots (approx. 350g/12½oz)

¼ red cabbage (approx. 200g/7oz)

¼ white cabbage (approx 250g/9oz)

5 spring onions (scallions), finely sliced

1 Tbsp sesame oil

2 Tbsp white vinegar

1 Tbsp soy sauce

2.5cm (1in) ginger, finely grated

1 clove garlic, finely grated

1 Tbsp sesame seeds

sea salt

cut

Slice the carrots into fine matchsticks. Slice the cabbages and spring onions finely. Place all the vegetables into a large bowl.

mix

Make the dressing by combining the sesame oil, white vinegar, soy sauce, ginger, garlic and sesame seeds in a small bowl and whisk well.

dress

Tip over the sliced vegetables, taste and season with sea salt as needed.

pa muchim

(spring onion salad)

serves 4

prep

ingredients
6 spring onions (scallions), very
finely sliced lengthways

1 Tbsp sesame oil
1 Tbsp soy sauce
1 Tbsp rice vinegar
1 Tbsp gochugaru
1 tsp caster (superfine) sugar
1 tsp sesame seeds

place
Place the sliced spring onions in a bowl of very
cold water and leave to sit for 15 minutes. This
will help them to crisp up.

mix
Make the dressing by mixing the sesame oil, soy
sauce, rice vinegar, gochugaru, sugar and sesame
seeds together.

serve
Drain the spring onions well and dress just
before serving.

20 namul
(seasoned vegetables)

serves ●●

prep ▶

cook /

ingredients

200g (7oz) baby spinach
1 clove garlic, very finely
  chopped
1 spring onion (scallion),
  very finely chopped
2 Tbsp sesame seeds
1 Tbsp sesame oil
2 Tbsp soy sauce, plus extra
  to serve
1 tsp gochujang, optional, to
  serve

boil

Bring a large pan of salted water to the boil and
drop in the spinach. Cook for 10–20 seconds, until
just wilted, then drain in a colander, shaking well.
With kitchen paper, gently squeeze the spinach to
remove any excess water.

mix

Mix the garlic, spring onion, sesame seeds,
sesame oil and soy sauce in a bowl, then
gently stir through the spinach. Taste and season
with more soy sauce, and serve hot. For a spicier
version of this dish, add a teaspoon of gochujang
into the mix.

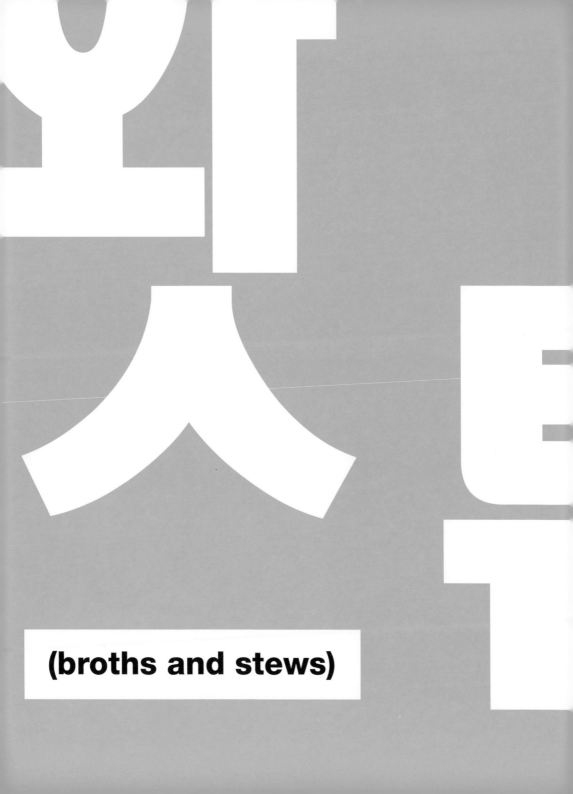

(broths and stews)

gamjatang

(pork broth)

ingredients

1.3kg (2lb 14oz) pork neck
   bones or ribs
5cm (2in) ginger, half sliced and
   the rest finely chopped
6 cloves garlic, roughly chopped
1 onion, roughly chopped
2 Tbsp doenjang
500g (1lb 2oz) potatoes, cut into
   2.5-cm (1-in) cubes
300g (10½oz) napa cabbage,
   cut into 2.5-cm (1-in) pieces
300g (10½oz) beansprouts
5–6 perilla leaves
freshly ground black pepper

4 cloves garlic, finely chopped
1 heaped Tbsp gochugaru
2 Tbsp gochujang
4 Tbsp mirin
4 Tbsp fish sauce
1 Tbsp perilla seeds, ground

soak

Cover the pork bones with water in a large bowl,
and soak for 1–2 hours. Transfer to a stockpot and
cover with fresh water, then bring to the boil. Add
the ginger slices and boil rapidly for 5 minutes.

drain

Remove from the heat, drain and rinse the bones.
Return the bones to the pot with 2.5 litres (85fl
oz/10 cups) water, the garlic, onion, doenjang and
the chopped ginger. Bring to the boil, then reduce
the heat to low and simmer, partially covered,
for 2 hours.

mix

For the paste mix together the garlic, gochugaru,
gochujang, mirin, fish sauce and perilla seeds.

add

Add the potatoes to the soup along with the
garlic chilli paste for the last 30 minutes, and the
cabbage, beansprouts and perilla leaves for the
final 10 minutes. Serve hot, with freshly ground
black pepper.

haemul jeongol
(seafood stew)

serves

prep

cook

ingredients

1 Tbsp vegetable oil
1 onion, finely sliced
5cm (2in) ginger, minced
3 cloves garlic, minced
2 Tbsp gochujang
2 Tbsp gochugaru
2 Tbsp fish sauce
2 Tbsp soy sauce
2.5 litres (85fl oz/10 cups)
   vegetable stock
180g (6½oz) king prawns
500g (1lb 2oz) mussels
300g (10½oz) squid rings
200g (7oz) napa cabbage,
   chopped into 2.5-cm
   (1-in) pieces

2 spring onions (scallions),
   finely sliced, to serve

heat

Heat the vegetable oil in a large saucepan and add the onion, ginger and garlic. Stir-fry for 5–6 minutes, until just softened but not coloured.

stir

Stir through the gochujang, gochugaru, fish sauce and soy sauce and mix well. Pour in the vegetable stock, bring to the boil and then simmer for 20 minutes.

simmer

Add the prawns, mussels, squid rings and napa cabbage, and simmer very gently for a further 3 minutes until the mussels open. Serve immediately, scattered with the spring onions.

kimchi jjigae

(tofu stew)

serves ●●●●

prep

cook

ingredients

1 Tbsp vegetable oil
250g (9oz) kimchi (see page 38),
   roughly chopped
1 onion, finely chopped
1 clove garlic, minced
2.5cm (1in) ginger, minced
1 Tbsp gochugaru
1 tsp gochujang
120g (4½oz) fresh shiitake
   mushrooms, halved
2 tsp sea salt
freshly ground black pepper
220g (8oz) firm tofu

1 spring onion (scallion), finely
   sliced, to serve

fry

Heat the vegetable oil in a large saucepan, add the
kimchi, onion, garlic and ginger, and stir-fry for
5 minutes.

mix

Stir through the gochugaru and gochujang, then
add the mushrooms, 2 litres (68 fl oz/8 cups)
water, sea salt and a good grind of black pepper.
Bring to the boil and simmer, uncovered, for 25
minutes.

slice

Slice the tofu into 1-cm (½-in) slices. After the
mixture has cooked for 20 minutes, taste it and
adjust the level of salt if needed. Place the tofu
on top of it, spoon some of the sauce over it, and
cook gently for a further 5 minutes. Top with the
spring onion, and serve immediately.

24 manduguk
(dumpling soup)

serves ●●●●

prep ◐

cook ◑

ingredients

10 dried anchovies
3 cloves garlic, roughly chopped
3 spring onions (scallions),
   roughly chopped
1 small onion, roughly chopped
2 tsp salt

12 mandu, uncooked
   (see page 22–23)
1 egg, beaten

1 spring onion (scallion),
   finely sliced

boil

For the anchovy broth, heat 1.5 litres (51fl oz/6 cups) water, anchovies, garlic, spring onions, onion and salt in a large saucepan and bring to the boil.

simmer

Reduce the heat to a simmer and cook, uncovered, for 30 minutes. Strain the broth through a sieve into a clean pan and discard the vegetables.

season

Taste and season the broth with more salt as needed, then return it to the boil. Add the mandu to the pan and reduce the heat to a simmer. Cook for 6–7 minutes, until the mandu are cooked through and rise to the surface of the broth.

whisk

Divide the mandu between four bowls, then with the heat off, whisk the beaten egg through the broth. Pour the broth over the dumplings, scatter with spring onion, and serve immediately.

sam-gyetang

(chicken soup)

serves

prep

soak

cook

ingredients

100g (3½oz/½ cup)
   glutinous rice
4 jujubes (red dates)
2 ginseng roots, sliced
10 cloves garlic, peeled
2 poussins (approx. 500g/1lb
   2oz each)
2 spring onions (scallions),
   finely chopped
2.5cm (1in) ginger, finely sliced
salt and freshly ground black
   pepper

1 spring onion (scallion), finely
   sliced, to serve

rinse

Rinse the rice well, place in a bowl and cover with
cold water. Leave to soak for 1 hour along with the
jujubes.

arrange

Place one soaked jujube, a few slices of ginseng
root, 3 garlic cloves, the spring onions and a
quarter of the ginger into each poussin.

assemble

Drain the rice, then use it to top up the cavity of
each poussin. Make sure not to fill them any more
than one-third full, as you need to leave room for
the rice to expand as it cooks. Cross the poussin
legs over, and tie them together tightly with string.

➡➡➡
boil

Arrange the poussins in a large saucepan with the remaining rice, jujubes, ginseng, ginger and garlic. Cover with cold water, season well with sea salt and black pepper, then bring to the boil. Skim the scum from the surface of the broth, then reduce the heat and simmer, partially covered, for 40 minutes. Turn the chickens over halfway through cooking and remove the scum every 10 minutes or so.

season

Taste the broth and season as needed with more salt and pepper. Serve one poussin per person, along with the broth, and top with the finely sliced spring onion just before serving.

budae jjigae

(spam stew)

serves

prep

cook

ingredients

2 litres (68fl oz/8 cups) anchovy
   broth (see page 119) or fish stock
250g (9oz) kimchi (see page 38)
1 onion, finely chopped
2 cloves garlic, minced
5cm (2in) ginger, minced
1 Tbsp gochugaru
1 tsp gochujang
1 x 400g (14oz) tin baked
   beans, rinsed
1 x 340g (12oz) tin Spam, sliced
600g (1lb 5oz) hot dogs, sliced into
   1-cm (½-in) chunks
300g (10½oz) bacon, cut into
   2-cm (¾-in) pieces
200g (7oz) instant ramen noodles
soy sauce, to taste

2 spring onions (scallions), finely
   sliced, to serve

strain

Strain the anchovy broth into a large stockpot, and add the kimchi, onion, garlic, ginger, gochugaru and gochujang. Bring to the boil and simmer for 15 minutes.

stir

Stir through the baked beans, then add the sliced spam, hot dogs and bacon to the pan. Simmer for a further 10 minutes until the bacon and hot dogs are cooked through. Add the ramen noodles and simmer for another 2–3 minutes, until the noodles have softened.

season

Taste and season with soy sauce to taste, then serve scattered with the spring onions.

27

yukgae-jang

(shredded beef soup)

serves

prep

cook x2

ingredients

450g (1lb) beef brisket
1 small onion, halved
2 cloves garlic, smashed
5 Tbsp sesame oil
3 Tbsp gochugaru
2 cloves garlic, minced
2 Tbsp soy sauce
250g (9oz) daikon radish, cut
    into 1-cm (½-in) chunks
50g (1¾oz) dried gosari,
    rehydrated overnight in
    cold water
400g (14oz) beansprouts
3 spring onions (scallions),
    cut into 2.5-cm (1-in) lengths
sea salt

boil

Place the brisket, onion and garlic in a large stockpot with 2 litres (68fl oz/8 cups) water and bring to the boil. Reduce the heat to low and simmer for 1 hour 30 minutes. Discard the onion and garlic and transfer the beef to a plate. Shred when cool enough to handle.

cook

Mix 3 tablespoons of the sesame oil, 2 tablespoons of the gochugaru, garlic and soy sauce in a large bowl. Stir in the radish, gosari, beansprouts and shredded beef. Leave to sit for 10 minutes before returning to the broth. Bring to the boil, and simmer for 15 minutes before adding the spring onions and cooking for a further 5 minutes. As soon as the soup is cooked, heat the remaining sesame oil and gochugaru in a small frying pan for 1 minute, then tip it into the hot soup. Season to taste with sea salt and serve.

28 seolle-ongtang

(bone broth)

serves **6-8**

prep

cook **9+**

ingredients

1kg (2lb 3oz) oxtail
450g (1lb) beef brisket

hot cooked rice, to serve
4 spring onions (scallions),
   finely sliced, to serve
sea salt and freshly ground
   black pepper

soak

Place the oxtail in a bowl and cover with cold water.
Leave to soak for 15 minutes, then drain.

boil

Transfer the bones to a very large stockpot and cover
with 4–5 times their volume of cold water. Bring to the
boil and simmer for 10 minutes. Drain and rinse the
bones and discard the water, then return the bones
to a clean pan with the brisket.

skim

Cover the beef with 2 litres (68fl oz/10 cups) cold
water, then bring to the boil. Skim off the scum,
reduce the heat to a simmer, and cook for 3 hours,
partially covered, skimming the surface often.

drain

Remove the brisket and drain the broth into a large
bowl. Allow both the brisket and broth to cool to
room temperature, then refrigerate. Meanwhile, return
the bones to the pot with 2 litres (68fl oz/10 cups)
more water, bring to the boil, then simmer again,
partially covered, for 3 hours.

simmer

Add a further 1.5 litres (51fl oz/6 cups) water to
the pot and simmer for a further 3 hours. Discard
the bones, allow the broth to cool to room
temperature, and refrigerate. The next day, scoop
the fat from the top of both and discard. Ladle out
the broth into a saucepan as needed and reheat
until boiling. Serve with the sliced brisket, hot rice,
spring onions and salt and pepper.

외식 (big dishes)

KFC [Korean fried chicken]

ingredients

150g (5½oz/1¼ cups) plain (all-purpose) flour

150g (5½oz/1¼ cups) cornflour (cornstarch)

1 Tbsp salt

1 Tbsp freshly ground black pepper

5cm (2in) ginger, grated

2 cloves garlic, grated

2kg (4lb 6oz) free-range chicken thighs and drumsticks (skin on, bone in)

2 litres (68fl oz/8 cups) sunflower oil, to deep-fry

65g (2¼oz) gochujang

2 Tbsp brown sugar

2 Tbsp soy sauce

1 Tbsp sesame oil

1 Tbsp white vinegar

2.5cm (1in) ginger, grated

1 clove garlic, grated

1 tsp gochugaru

➡ ➡ ➡

mix

In a large roasting tin, mix together the flours, salt, black pepper, ginger and garlic. Tip in the chicken thighs and drumsticks, coat well in the flour mixture, and set aside for 20 minutes.

pour

Pour the oil into your largest, deepest pan, making sure to fill it no more than half full. Place on a low heat, and heat gently until it reaches 160°C/320°F.

heat

Make the sauce by combining the gochujang, brown sugar, soy sauce, sesame oil, white vinegar, ginger, garlic and gochugaru in a small saucepan over a low heat. Stir frequently until the mixture comes to the boil, then simmer for 2 minutes until glossy and sticky. Turn off the heat.

fry

Once the oil has reached 160°C/320°F, carefully lower in five or six pieces of chicken, shaking off the excess flour first, and deep-fry for 12 minutes.

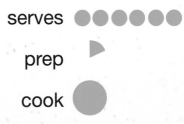

serves ●●●●●●

prep ▶

cook ●

➡➡➡
equipment
a thermometer

Remove carefully with tongs and transfer to a wire rack, then repeat until all the chicken is cooked. (This will take three batches of cooking – do not overcrowd the pan or you'll run the risk of the oil boiling over.) For the second round of frying, heat the oil to 180°C/350°F. Carefully lower in five or six pieces of chicken at a time, and fry for a further 10 minutes per batch, transferring the cooked chicken onto a baking (sheet) tray lined with kitchen paper as you go. To keep the chicken hot, pop the baking (sheet) tray into an oven preheated to 100°C/200°F as you go. Continue until all the chicken has been fried twice.

serve
When all the chicken is cooked, reheat the sauce, and pour it into a large bowl. Toss the fried chicken pieces in the sauce and serve immediately.

30

bulgogi
(marinated beef)

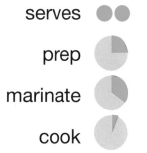

serves

prep

marinate

cook

ingredients

2 sirloin steaks (approx. 220g/8oz each)

2 Tbsp soy sauce

30g (1oz) brown sugar

2.5cm (1in) ginger, minced

3 cloves garlic, minced

½ onion, finely chopped

2 spring onions (scallions), finely chopped

1 small pear or apple, finely grated

1 Tbsp sesame oil

1 tsp freshly ground black pepper

1 Tbsp sesame oil

4 Tbsp doenjang

2 Tbsp gochujang

1 spring onion (scallion), finely chopped

1 Tbsp mirin

1 tsp honey

1 tsp toasted sesame seeds

1 Tbsp sesame seeds, to serve

cos (romaine) lettuce leaves, to serve

1 large carrot, peeled and cut into matchsticks, to serve

½ cucumber, cut into matchsticks, to serve

cut

Trim the fat from the steaks, and thinly slice into 2mm (1/12 in) strips. Set aside in a bowl.

mix

Mix together the soy sauce, brown sugar, ginger, garlic, onion, spring onions, grated pear, sesame oil and pepper in a small bowl. Add to the beef and stir well. Leave to marinate for 15–20 minutes.

mix

Meanwhile, make the ssamjang sauce by mixing together the sesame oil, doenjang, gochujang, spring onion, mirin, honey and sesame seeds.

heat

Heat a large frying pan or wok until smoking. Place the marinated beef in a colander, and give it a good shake to remove the excess marinade. Tip it carefully into the smoking hot wok, and stir-fry for 2 minutes for a medium steak or 3–4 minutes for a well done one.

serve

Scatter the beef with the sesame seeds and serve immediately with the lettuce leaves, ssamjang sauce for dipping and carrot and cucumber sticks.

31

chicken bulgogi

(barbecued chicken)

serves

prep

marinate **2+**

cook

ingredients

2 Tbsp soy sauce
1 Tbsp sesame oil
1 Tbsp rice wine
juice of ½ lemon
1 Tbsp brown sugar
1 spring onion (scallion),
   finely chopped
2 cloves garlic, minced
2.5cm (1in) ginger, minced
1 tsp sesame seeds
large pinch freshly ground
   black pepper
400g (14oz) skinless, boneless
   chicken thighs, halved

1 spring onion (scallion), finely
   chopped, to serve
2 cos (romaine) lettuces,
   leaves picked, to serve

mix

Mix together the soy sauce, sesame oil, rice
wine, lemon juice, sugar, spring onion, garlic,
ginger, sesame seeds and black pepper in a large
bowl. Add the chicken and mix well. Cover and
refrigerate for 2 hours, or preferably overnight.

fry

Heat a griddle pan until smoking, then add the
chicken pieces in a single layer. You may need to
do this in two batches, depending on the size of
your griddle. Cook for 5–6 minutes on each side,
until cooked through, then transfer to a plate.

Tip the remaining marinade into a small saucepan,
and bubble down for 5 minutes until reduced.
Brush this mixture over the chicken as it cooks.
Serve the chicken hot, scattered with the spring
onion, and lettuce leaves.

32

bulgalbi
(barbecued ribs)

serves

prep

marinate **over-night**

cook

ingredients

1.5kg (3lb 5oz) beef short ribs,
cut into 5-cm (2-in) chunks

100ml (3½fl oz/½ cup)
soy sauce
2 Tbsp rice vinegar
2 Tbsp sesame oil
2 cloves garlic, minced
2.5cm (1in) ginger, minced
2 spring onions (scallions),
finely chopped
1 Tbsp caster (superfine) sugar

cos (romaine) lettuce cups and
ssamjang sauce (see page
85), to serve

cut

Place the ribs on a large chopping board. With a
very sharp knife, carefully cut towards the bone,
then fillet around it so that you have one long
strip of meat, with the bone attached at one end.
Continue until all the ribs are butterflied.

mix

Make the marinade by mixing together the soy
sauce, rice vinegar, sesame oil, garlic, ginger,
spring onions and sugar in a large bowl. Place the
prepared ribs in the marinade, mix well, then cover
and refrigerate overnight.

heat

Just before you are ready to eat, heat a
heavy-based griddle pan until smoking hot.
Tip the marinated meat into a colander set over
a bowl and shake well to remove the excess
marinade. Working in batches, place the strips of
meat onto the griddle, and cook for 4 minutes per
side until charred. (You can also cook these on
a very hot barbecue, following the same cooking
times.) Transfer to a plate and cover loosely with
aluminum foil while you continue with the rest of
the meat.

serve

Serve hot with the lettuce cups and the
ssamjang sauce.

galbijjim

(beef stew)

ingredients

1.5kg (3lb 5oz) beef short ribs
5 dried shiitake mushrooms
1 onion, roughly sliced
6 cloves garlic, peeled
5cm (2in) ginger, peeled and
   roughly sliced
4 Tbsp soy sauce
4 tsp mirin
2 Tbsp brown sugar
200g (7oz) carrots, cut into
   2-cm (¾-in) slices
200g (7oz) potatoes or Korean
   radish, cut into 2-cm
   (¾-in) chunks
1 spring onion (scallion), finely
   sliced
8 jujubes (red dates)

soak

Place the ribs in a bowl of 1.5 litres (51fl oz/6 cups) cold water and soak for 30–40 minutes, changing the water once. Soak the shiitake mushrooms in a bowl of just-boiled water for 1 hour.

boil

Transfer the ribs to a stockpot, cover with fresh cold water and bring to the boil. Rapidly boil for 5 minutes. Drain and rinse the ribs, then return them to the pot. Pour in a further 1.5 litres (51fl oz/6 cups) of cold water, add the onion, garlic, ginger, soy sauce, mirin and brown sugar. Bring to the boil, then simmer for 30 minutes.

add

Add the carrots, potatoes and rehydrated mushrooms, then simmer, uncovered, for a further hour. Add the spring onion and jujubes for the last 10 minutes. Serve the meat and vegetables divided between four bowls, with the cooking broth poured over.

bossam
(pork belly)

serves

prep

cook **x2**

ingredients
1kg (2lb 3oz) pork belly (side)
10 cloves garlic, crushed
100g (3¼oz) ginger, thinly sliced
1 onion, roughly sliced
2 tsp sea salt
1 tsp black peppercorns
70g (2½oz) doenjang
80ml (2½fl oz/⅓ cup) rice wine

1 Tbsp sesame oil
1 tsp saeujeot
1 Tbsp gochugaru
1 spring onion (scallion),
   finely sliced
1 tsp sesame seeds

lettuce leaves, to serve
kimchi (see page 38), to serve

boil
Preheat your oven to 150°C/300°F. Place the pork, garlic, ginger, onion, salt and black peppercorns in an ovenproof stockpot large enough to hold the pork comfortably. Whisk together the doenjang and the rice wine until smooth, and tip it into the pot along with 1.5 litres (51fl oz/6 cups) cold water. Bring to the boil, then transfer to the oven to cook for 2 hours.

mix
Meanwhile, make the shrimp sauce by whisking together the sesame oil, 2 tablespoons water, saeujeot, gochugaru, spring onion and sesame seeds, and set aside.

slice
Once cooked, remove the pork from the liquid, and pat dry. Thinly slice and arrange on a platter with the lettuce, shrimp sauce and kimchi, and let everyone make their own wraps at the table.

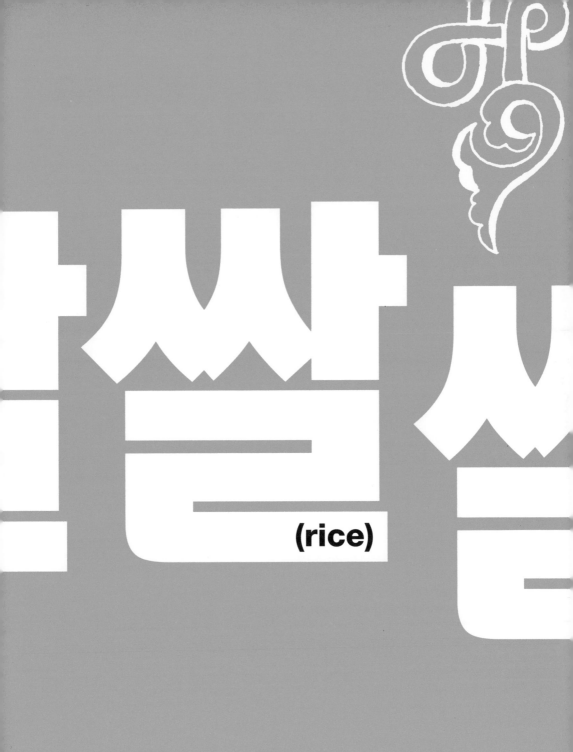

쌀

(rice)

35

bibimbap

(rice with beef
and vegetables)

serves

prep

cook

ingredients

1 red (bell) pepper
150g (5½oz) mushrooms
120g (4½oz/⅔ cup) short-grain
   white rice
4 Tbsp sesame oil
250g (9oz) minced
   (ground) beef
sea salt
100g (3½oz) spinach
2 free-range eggs
1 tsp vegetable oil

2.5cm (1in) ginger, grated
1 clove garlic, grated
2 Tbsp white vinegar
2 Tbsp gochujang
pinch caster (superfine) sugar

prepare

Preheat your oven to 100ºC/200ºF. Finely
cut the red pepper into matchsticks and
slice the mushrooms.

boil

Rinse the rice, tip into a large pan of boiling salted
water, and cook for 12–13 minutes before draining.
Return to the pan, cover and allow to steam dry for
10 minutes.

fry

Heat 1 tablespoon of the sesame oil in a large
frying pan and add the beef. Stir-fry for 5 minutes
until cooked through and well broken up, season
with a good pinch of salt, then tip onto a plate and
place in the oven to keep warm.

heat

Heat another tablespoon of sesame oil in the same pan, and stir-fry the pepper matchsticks for 5 minutes, seasoning with a pinch of sea salt, before tipping these onto a plate and placing in the oven along with the beef.

fry

Heat another tablespoon of the sesame oil and stir-fry the mushrooms for 5 minutes. Season with sea salt, and transfer to the oven with the pepper.

heat

Heat the final tablespoon of sesame oil and wilt the spinach for 1–2 minutes. Season and pop onto the plate in the oven alongside the beef.

mix

Meanwhile, make the sauce by mixing together the ginger, garlic, vinegar and gochujang. Taste and season with a pinch of sugar if required.

serve

Just before serving, fry the eggs in a teaspoon of vegetable oil for 3 minutes, or until cooked to your liking. Pile the hot rice into bowls, arrange the beef and vegetables on top, finish with a fried egg and serve with the sauce alongside.

36 vegetarian bibimbap

(rice with vegetables)

serves

prep

cook

ingredients

200g (7oz/1 cup) short-grain
white rice
2 cloves garlic, finely minced
5cm (2in) ginger, finely minced
4 Tbsp sesame oil
220g (8oz) firm tofu, cut into
1-cm (½-in) slices
1 red (bell) pepper, finely sliced
120g (4oz) fresh shiitake
mushrooms
100g (3½oz) spinach
sea salt
2 fried eggs

1 quantity of bibimbap sauce
(see page 98)

boil

Rinse the rice, tip into a large pan of boiling salted
water and cook for 12–13 minutes before draining.
Return to the pan, cover and allow to steam dry for
10 minutes.

mix

Mix together the garlic and ginger in a small bowl.
Heat 1 tablespoon of sesame oil in a large frying
pan, and add one-quarter of the garlic and ginger
mixture. Stir-fry for a few seconds, add the tofu,
then fry for 4 minutes per side until golden. Transfer
to a plate.

fry

Add another tablespoon of sesame oil and another
quarter of the ginger and garlic. Stir-fry the pepper
for 3 minutes, until just softened. Season, then
transfer to a plate. Repeat this process with the
mushrooms and spinach, tipping onto a plate
after each is done. Divide the rice between bowls,
arrange the vegetables and tofu on top. Finish with
a fried egg and serve with the sauce alongside.

37

deopbap
(calamari rice)

serves

prep

marinate

cook

ingredients

100g (3½oz/½ cup) white rice
1 Tbsp gochugaru
2 Tbsp gochujang
2 Tbsp soy sauce
2 spring onions (scallions),
   finely sliced
2 cloves garlic, minced
2.5cm (1in) ginger, minced
200g (7oz) calamari
1 Tbsp vegetable oil
1 carrot, peeled and cut into
   matchsticks

rinse

Rinse the rice, tip into a large pan of boiling salted water and cook for 12–13 minutes before draining. Return to the pan, cover and allow to steam dry for 10 minutes.

mix

Meanwhile, mix the gochugaru, gochujang, soy sauce, spring onions, garlic and ginger together in a bowl, then stir through the calamari. Cover and leave to marinate for 15 minutes.

heat

Heat the vegetable oil in a small wok or frying pan, and add the carrot. Stir-fry for 3 minutes, then add the calamari, and continue to stir-fry for a further 3–4 minutes until the calamari is cooked through. Serve over the hot rice.

38

kimchi
bokke-
umbap

(kimchi fried rice)

serves ●●

prep

cook

ingredients

200g (7oz/1 cup) short-grain
  white rice
2 Tbsp vegetable oil
250g (9oz) kimchi (see page 38),
  chopped into 1-cm
  (½-in) chunks
2 Tbsp sesame oil
2 Tbsp soy sauce
sea salt
2 spring onions (scallions),
  finely chopped
2 fried eggs (optional), to serve

rinse

Rinse the rice in plenty of cold running water, then
place in a saucepan. Cover with 5–6 times its
volume in cold water, then bring to the boil. Simmer
for 15–20 minutes, until the rice is cooked through,
then drain well.

heat

Heat the vegetable oil in a large frying pan or wok
and fry the kimchi for 2–3 minutes. Add the cooked
rice, sesame oil and soy sauce, and stir-fry for a
further 2–3 minutes. Season to taste with more soy
sauce or sea salt as needed.

stir

Stir through the spring onions, and serve hot, with
a fried egg on top if you wish.

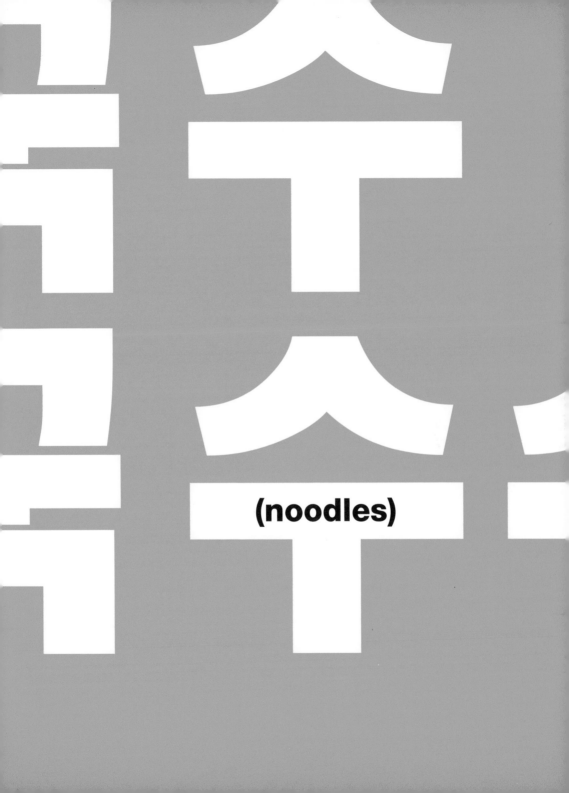

(noodles)

jajang-
myeon

(black bean noodles)

ingredients

400g (14oz) pork loin/fillet, cut
 into 2-cm (¾-in) chunks
2 Tbsp rice wine
1 tsp sea salt
3 Tbsp vegetable oil
1 onion, finely chopped
1 courgette (zucchini) (approx.
 125g/4½oz), cut into 1-cm
 (½-in) chunks
1 potato (approx. 125g/4½oz),
 cut into 1-cm (½-in) chunks
200g (7oz) black bean paste
2 Tbsp brown sugar
300ml (10fl oz/1¼ cups)
 chicken stock
400g (14oz) jajangmyeon or
 udon noodles
1 Tbsp cornflour (cornstarch)

1 spring onion (scallion) or
 ¼ cucumber, finely sliced,
 to serve

marinate

Mix the pork, rice wine and sea salt together in a
bowl, and leave to marinate for 20 minutes.

fry

Heat 2 tablespoons of the vegetable oil in a
large frying pan or wok and add the onion,
courgette and potato. Stir-fry for 5 minutes on a
medium heat, then tip onto a plate. Heat another
tablespoon of oil and stir-fry the pork on a medium
to high heat for 5 minutes until lightly browned.
Return the vegetables to the pan, along with the
black bean paste. Stir-fry over a medium heat for
3–4 minutes, then add the sugar and chicken
stock. Stir well, then simmer for 10 minutes.

boil

Meanwhile, boil the noodles in a pan of water
according to the packet instructions. Drain and
set aside.

serves ●●●●

prep ◗

marinate ◗

cook ◗

mix
Mix the cornflour with 2 tablespoons cold water until smooth and add this to the sauce for the final 2 minutes of cooking, stirring continuously until thickened and glossy.

serve
Serve the pork and sauce over the noodles, and top with the spring onion or cucumber.

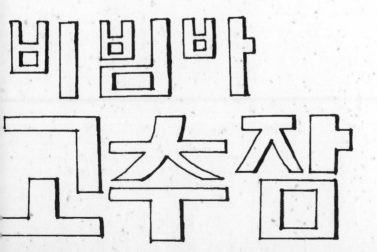

japchae
(sweet potato noodles)

serves ●●

prep

cook

ingredients

200g (7oz) sweet
   potato or glass noodles
3 Tbsp sesame oil
4 Tbsp soy sauce
3 Tbsp vegetable oil
100g (3½oz) spinach,
   finely sliced
1 red (bell) pepper, finely sliced
1 carrot, peeled and cut into
   matchsticks
120g (4½oz) fresh shiitake
   mushrooms, finely sliced
200g (7oz) sirloin steak,
   finely sliced
2 spring onions (scallions),
   finely sliced
1 clove garlic, minced
1 Tbsp sesame seeds
sea salt and freshly ground
   black pepper

boil

Bring a large pan of water to the boil and add
the noodles. Simmer for 6–7 minutes, until just
cooked, then drain. Stir through 1 tablespoon
of the sesame oil along with 1 tablespoon of
the soy sauce.

heat

Heat ½ tablespoon vegetable oil in a frying pan or
wok and stir-fry the spinach for barely a minute,
until just wilted. Set aside.

stir-fry

Add a tablespoon of vegetable oil to the wok, and
stir-fry the pepper for 2 minutes on a high heat with
a pinch of salt. Set aside. Repeat, stir-frying the
carrot, mushrooms, steak and spring onions, one
by one, for 2 minutes each, adding more oil to the
pan as needed and a pinch of salt to each.

mix

Make the dressing by combining the remaining
sesame oil and soy sauce with the garlic, sesame
seeds and a good grind of black pepper.

add

Once all the vegetables and steak are cooked,
add them to the noodles along with the dressing,
and return to the wok for a further minute to heat
through. Season to taste as needed with more soy
sauce or sea salt and serve immediately.

naeng-myeon
(cold noodles)

serves ●●●●

prep ◑

cook x2

ingredients

400g (14oz) beef brisket
1 onion, roughly sliced
5cm (2in) ginger, roughly
    chopped
6 cloves garlic, halved
150g (5½oz) daikon radish,
    roughly sliced
2 tsp sea salt
1 tsp black peppercorns

2 Tbsp gochugaru
1 Tbsp gochujang
2 Tbsp soy sauce
1 clove garlic, minced
2.5cm (1in) ginger, minced
1 spring onion (scallion), finely
    chopped
1 Tbsp sesame oil
1 tsp sesame seeds

400g (14oz) buckwheat noodles
2 eggs
½ cucumber, cut into
    matchsticks, to serve
1 Korean pear, finely sliced,
    to serve

boil

First make the broth: place the brisket, onion,
ginger, garlic, daikon radish, sea salt and
peppercorns in a large stockpot along with 2 litres
(68fl oz/8 cups) cold water. Bring to the boil, then
lower the heat and simmer, partially covered, for 1
hour 30 minutes.

mix

Meanwhile, make the sauce by mixing the
gochugaru, gochujang, soy sauce, garlic, ginger,
spring onion, sesame oil and sesame seeds
together in a bowl.

strain

Remove the brisket from the broth and strain
the broth through a sieve into a jug. Discard the
vegetables. Taste and season, then allow the broth
and brisket to cool to room temperature. Chill in the
fridge until ready to serve.

cook

When ready to serve, bring a large pan of water to
the boil, add the buckwheat noodles and whole
eggs. Cook the noodles for for 4–5 minutes (or
according to the packet instructions), then lift into
a colander and drain. Rinse well in cold water.
Remove the eggs after 7 minutes and allow to
cool before peeling and halving.

serve

To serve, slice the brisket, and divide between
bowls along with the noodles and broth. Top
each bowl with half an egg. Serve cold with
cucumber and pear.

janchi guksu

(feast noodles)

serves

prep

cook

ingredients

1 onion, roughly sliced
1 spring onion (scallion),
  roughly sliced
3 cloves garlic, roughly chopped
15 dried anchovies
5g (¼oz) dried kelp/seaweed,
  broken into pieces
250g (9oz) Korean radish,
  roughly chopped
sea salt

500g (1lb 2oz) somen noodles
2 Tbsp sesame oil
1 large courgette (zucchini), cut
  into matchsticks
1 large carrot, peeled and cut
  into matchsticks
2 eggs, lightly beaten
2 spring onions (scallions), finely
  sliced, to serve

1 Tbsp sesame oil
40g (1½oz) kimchi (see page
  38), finely chopped
1 Tbsp gochujang
1 Tbsp gochugaru
1 spring onion (scallion),
  finely sliced

boil

For the anchovy broth, place the onion, spring onion, garlic, dried anchovies, seaweed and Korean radish in a large stockpot with 2.5 litres (85fl oz/10 cups) water. Bring to the boil, reduce the heat and simmer for 30 minutes. Season to taste with the sea salt, then strain through a sieve into a jug and discard the vegetables, reserving the stock.

mix

Meanwhile, make the kimchi sauce by mixing the sesame oil, kimchi, gochujang, gochugaru and spring onion together in a small bowl. Set aside.

boil

Cook the noodles in a pan of boiling water for 2 minutes until still slightly *al dente* (or according to the packet instructions), then drain.

fry

Heat ½ tablespoon sesame oil in a frying pan or wok, and stir-fry the courgette for 2 minutes. Set aside, and repeat with the carrot, then set aside. Finally add the eggs to make a thin omelette, cooking it for 2 minutes on each side or until just set. Transfer to a plate and slice the omelette into thin strips.

serve

Divide the noodles between two serving bowls, and pour over the hot broth. Top with the vegetables and omelette strips. Serve with the spring onions and the kimchi sauce alongside.

43

jaengban guksu

(cold noodle salad)

serves

prep

cook

ingredients

150g (5½oz) soba noodles
2 Tbsp sesame oil
3 eggs
1 carrot, cut into thin strips
¼ white cabbage approx. 200–250g (7–9oz), finely shredded
½ cucumber, deseeded and cut into thin strips
¼ red cabbage, approx. 200–250g (7–9oz), finely shredded
50g (1¾oz) sprouted seeds

3 Tbsp soy sauce
1 clove garlic, grated
2 Tbsp vinegar
1 Tbsp gochujang
1 Tbsp gochugaru
1 tsp sesame seeds
1 tsp caster (superfine) sugar

boil

Bring a large pan of salted water to the boil and cook the soba noodles for 5 minutes (or according to the packet instructions). Remove with tongs, drain in a colander and rinse in cold water, then mix with 1 tablespoon sesame oil in a bowl. Boil the eggs in the same pan for 10 minutes.

whisk

Meanwhile make the dressing by whisking the soy sauce, garlic, vinegar, gochujang, gochugaru, sesame seeds, sugar and remaining sesame oil in a bowl. Adjust the seasoning with soy sauce and vinegar, adding a little water to loosen the dressing.

serve

Remove the cooked eggs to a bowl of cold water, and leave for 5 minutes before peeling and slicing in half. Arrange the vegetables around a platter with the noodles in the middle. Top with the halved eggs and serve the dressing alongside.

jjampong

(spicy seafood noodles)

serves

prep

cook

ingredients

2 Tbsp vegetable oil
2 cloves garlic, minced
5cm (2in) ginger, minced
1 onion, finely sliced
300g (10½oz) pork belly
    (side), diced
200g (7oz) napa cabbage,
    finely sliced
1 carrot, peeled and cut into
    matchsticks
2 Tbsp gochugaru
1 Tbsp fish sauce
2 litres (68fl oz/8 cups) anchovy
    broth (see page 119) or
    fish stock
250g (9oz) raw udon noodles
400g (14oz) mixed seafood
    (squid, prawns [shrimp],
    mussels)
2 spring onions (scallions),
    finely sliced
sea salt

fry

Heat the vegetable oil in a large wok or frying pan, and add the garlic, ginger and onion. Stir-fry for 2–3 minutes, then add the pork and stir-fry for a further 5 minutes.

add

Add the napa cabbage and carrot and stir-fry for a further 2–3 minutes before stirring through the gochugaru and fish sauce. Pour in 1.5 litres (51fl oz/6 cups) of the anchovy broth and simmer for 10 minutes. Add the udon noodles and increase the heat for 5 minutes, then add the seafood.

simmer

Lower the heat and simmer for another 3 minutes, until the seafood is cooked through. Taste and season with sea salt as needed. Serve with the spring onions. If you are not serving the soup immediately, the noodles will absorb most of the broth, so add in the reserved 500ml (17fl oz/2 cups) of stock if needed.

bibim guksu

(spicy cold noodles)

serves

prep

cook

ingredients

1 egg
200g (7oz) somen noodles
50g (1¾oz) kimchi
    (see page 38)
50g (1¾oz) cucumber, cut
    into matchsticks
50g (1¾oz) carrot, peeled and
    cut into matchsticks

2 Tbsp gochujang
1 Tbsp gochugaru
2 Tbsp soy sauce
2 Tbsp rice vinegar
1 tsp honey
1 clove garlic, minced
1 tsp sesame seeds

boil

Bring a large pan of water to the boil and add the egg. Simmer for 7 minutes.

mix

Meanwhile, make the sauce by mixing the gochujang, gochugaru, soy sauce, rice vinegar, honey, garlic and sesame seeds for the sauce together in a bowl, and set aside.

peel

Remove the egg from the water using a slotted spoon and transfer to a bowl of cold water, before peeling and halving.

serve

Bring the water in the pan back to the boil, add the noodles and cook for 2 minutes before draining. Top with the sauce, kimchi, cucumber, carrot and egg, and serve immediately.

jatguksu
(noodles in pine nut broth)

serves

prep

chill

cook

ingredients

100g (3½oz/⅔ cup) pine nuts
1 tsp salt
200g (7oz) buckwheat or
  soba noodles
100g (3½oz) cucumber, cut
  into long matchsticks

2 tsp black sesame seeds,
  to serve

fry

Toast the pine nuts in a heavy-based frying pan, and on a very low heat, for 5–10 minutes, shaking the pan frequently, until barely golden. Transfer the pine nuts to a blender with the salt and 350ml (12fl oz/1½ cups) water, and blitz until completely smooth. Refrigerate for 30 minutes until well chilled.

boil

Bring a large pan of water to the boil, add the noodles and boil for 5 minutes (or according to the packet instructions), until just cooked. Drain and rinse well.

serve

Divide the noodles between four bowls and top with the cucumber. Pour over the pine nut broth, scatter over the sesame seeds and serve.

미지![

(desserts)

hwajeon

(Korean rice cakes)

serves **8**

prep

cook

ingredients

90g (3oz/generous ⅓ cup)
  caster (superfine) sugar
200g (7oz/1⅔ cups) glutinous/
  sweet rice flour
¼ tsp salt
2 Tbsp vegetable oil
16 edible flowers (e.g. violas)

heat

Place the sugar and 150ml (5fl oz/⅔ cup) water
in a small saucepan and heat until the sugar has
just dissolved.

mix

Mix the flour and salt together in a bowl and pour
the sugar syrup over it. Stir together with a fork and
then briefly knead with your hands to form a soft
dough. You may wish to lightly flour your hands if
the dough is initially too sticky.

divide

Divide the dough in half, and then in half again
and so on, until you have 16 portions. Cover the
portions in clingfilm (plastic wrap) while you work,
so that the dough does not dry out. Roll each
into a ball, and then flatten until you have a small
round, about 4.5cm (1¾in) in diameter, and
1cm (½in) in depth.

heat

Heat 1 tablespoon vegetable oil in a large frying
pan and press a small edible flower onto the top of
each rice cake. Carefully invert the rice cakes into
the pan, with the flower underneath, and fry for 2
minutes on a low heat. Flip the cakes over, and fry
for a further 2 minutes before transferring to a plate
lined with kitchen paper.

repeat

Repeat with the remaining hwajeon. These are
delicious served warm.

48 hotteok

(street food pancake)

serves ●●●●

prep

rise **x2**

cook

ingredients

250g (9oz/2 cups) plain
   (all-purpose) flour
½ tsp salt
2 tsp fast-action dried yeast
1 tsp caster (superfine) sugar

50g (1¾oz/⅓ cup) brown sugar
25g (1oz/¼ cup) walnuts,
   roughly chopped
½ tsp cinnamon powder

2 Tbsp vegetable oil, to fry

mix

Mix together the flour and salt in a large bowl. In
a jug, whisk together the yeast, sugar and 125ml
(4fl oz/½ cup) warm water, then pour into the flour.
Work together briefly into a sticky dough, then leave
to rise for 2 hours, or until doubled in size.

Meanwhile, make the filling by mixing together the
brown sugar, walnuts and cinnamon powder for the
filling and set aside.

divide

When the dough has risen, knock it back and leave
for a further 20 minutes. Divide the dough into
eight equal portions. Flatten each into a round, and
place a tablespoon of the walnut filling in the centre
of each. Fold up the corners and press down to
enclose the filling completely, patting it gently into
a 7-cm (2¾-in) circle. Repeat with the rest of the
dough and filling.

fry

Heat 1 tablespoon of the vegetable oil in a heavy-
based frying pan, and carefully place four hotteok
into the pan, pressing the dough down lightly with
a spatula as you go. Fry for 1 minute on a medium
heat, until golden-brown, and then flip them over.
Press down lightly again, and fry for a further
minute until golden-brown on both sides.

Transfer to a plate lined with kitchen paper while
you continue with the rest of the hotteok, and
serve warm.

patbingsu
(ice dessert)

serves

prep

ingredients
4 heaped Tbsp crushed ice
3 Tbsp condensed milk
2 Tbsp prepared sweet adzuki
beans (available from Asian
supermarkets)
2 strawberries, quartered
½ kiwi fruit, chopped
1 Tbsp patbingsu tteok (soft,
mini rice cakes for patbingsu)

pile
Pile the crushed ice into each glass, and pour over the condensed milk.

spoon
Spoon over the adzuki beans, strawberries, kiwis and patbingsu tteok, and serve immediately.

50

matang

(candied sweet potato)

serves ●●●●

prep

cook

ingredients

600g (1lb 5oz) sweet potato,
    peeled
1 Tbsp vegetable oil
150g (5½oz/generous ⅔ cup)
    caster (superfine) sugar
1 tsp black sesame seeds

500ml (17fl oz/generous 2 cups)
    vegetable oil, to fry

slice

Slice the sweet potato into 1-cm (½-in) rounds,
then across into halves.

fry

In a large saucepan, heat vegetable oil on a
medium heat until it reaches 180°C/350°F, or until
a cube of sweet potato dropped in starts bubbling
immediately on contact. Carefully lower in a third
of the sweet potato chunks. You will now need to
increase the heat, as the sweet potato will bring
the temperature down. Fry for 5–7 minutes until the
oil stops bubbling and the sweet potato is cooked
through. Transfer to a plate lined with kitchen paper,
and continue until the remaining the sweet potato
is cooked.

caramelise

In a large frying pan, heat 1 tablespoon of
vegetable oil and scatter with the sugar. Heat
without stirring on a low heat, until the sugar melts.
Increase the heat to medium and cook, until the
sugar begins to turn an amber colour – this will take
about 6 minutes. Instead of stirring, swirl the pan to
help the sugar caramelise evenly.

dip

Turn off the heat and, working with two sweet
potato pieces at a time, use a fork to dip them
into the hot caramel and then transfer to a plate.
Repeat until you have used up all the sweet
potato pieces and caramel, scattering each piece
immediately with the black sesame seeds. Leave
the caramel to set and eat while still warm.

index

publishing director: Sarah Lavelle
creative director: Helen Lewis
junior commissioning editor: Romilly Morgan
design and art direction: Claire Rochford
recipe developer and food stylist: Rukmini Iyer
designer: Gemma Hayden
photographer: Kim Lightbody
illustrator: Juriko Kosaka
prop stylist: Alexander Breeze
production controller: Tom Moore
production director: Vincent Smith

First published in 2016 by
Quadrille Publishing
Pentagon House
52–54 Southwark Street
London SE1 1UN
www.quadrille.co.uk
www.quadrille.com

Quadrille is an imprint of Hardie Grant
www.hardiegrant.com.au

Cataloguing in Publication Data: a catalogue record for this book is
available from the British Library.

ISBN: 978 184949 881 4

Printed in China

**Thank you to all the owners
and staff who allowed us to
shoot photographs in the
following locations: Centre
Point Food Store in New
Oxford Street WC1A, On the
Bab in Covent Garden WC2E**

Note: follow the standard safety
tips for deep frying – fill the pan no
more than half full with oil, keep
it towards the back of the stove,
do not leave it unattended, and
do not overcrowd the pan, or it
will bubble over. Once you have
finished frying, turn off the heat
and do not attempt to move the
pan of oil until it has completely
cooled down.